FAT BURNERS FREESTYLE 2018

By Olivia Brown

Delicious Freestyle Recipes For Rapid Fat Loss, The Proven Method To Stay Lean And Healthy

The information herein is offered for informational purposes solely, and is universal as so. The presentation of the information is without contract or any type of guarantee assurance.

The trademarks that are used are without any consent, and the publication of the trademark is without permission or backing by the trademark owner. All trademarks and brands within this book are for clarifying purposes only and are the owned by the owners themselves, not affiliated with this document.

Table of Contents

Introduction

Congratulation and thank you for your purchase of my book, *"Fat Burners Freestyle 2018:* **Delicious Freestyle Recipes For Rapid Fat Loss, The Proven Method To Stay Lean And Healthy**

This book contains proven steps and strategies on how to lose weight, and maintaining your health.

Weight watchers is tailored in a manner that makes it simpler for you to change your habits for the long-term. So, how much effort you will inject depends on how much you will have to alter your eating habits. This diet plan will also show you how to shop and cook healthy foods.

On this diet plan, the emphasis is on fruits and veggies because they are high in fiber and will keep you full.

As you struggle to lose weight, you may reach a stagnant stage. This is usually the time to make some changes. Even though adjusting your eating as well as exercising habits is not easy, you have to start somewhere. The best way in succeeding is making small changes. step by steps, like switching to fat-free or low-fat milk.

The Weight Watchers diet has been updated to its most optimal state as a Freestyle diet plan. Find out more about Zero points, and how this new measurement system is making all the difference.

Weight Watchers Freestyle is the newest plan. Change is just around the corner, with new daily points goals, food, rollover points, and more.

LOOK AT HOW ZERO POINTS WORK:

The biggest change to the diet plan is the new and innovative Zero Points. Although the old diet included fruits and veggies in adequate amounts, lean proteins are now added to the mix.

Various chicken types, such as skinless, lean ground and boneless chickens; skinless, thin sliced deli, lean ground, and boneless turkey; fresh seafoods, canned fish, tofu as well as eggs are now all foods classed as zero points.

Some foods have been reclassified based on their points. Non-dairy products such as yoghurt, soy yoghurt, as well as legumes are now worth nothing in Smartpoints values. Corn and Peas also were added to the Zero points values.

All Weight Watchers members will find this a welcome change, and the Zero points system is what many are most excited about. Legumes, fresh veggies, fresh fruits, as well as lean proteins are given a bigger focus in this new program structure. This continues to push members who are already using smartpoints to go even further, encouraging them to take up healthier choices and consume less foods that have a high degree of processing.

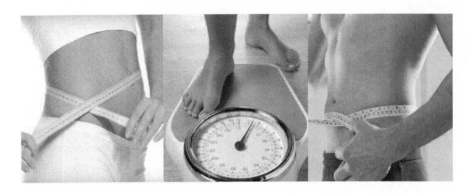

There are many programs that encourage dieting, but don't work as well compared with Zero points. Most will say the foods you can and can't eat, as well as the calories you ought to be taking in, including some restrictions intended to help, but are oftentimes frustrating to deal with. On the other hand if you use a points system, you don't have as many limits.

Your foods, your choice. There can be any number of food combinations you can eat, not restricting your diet pan to a few bland foods you'll bore of over time.

Weight watchers diet programs clinically supported to allow fast and effective weight loss, with the push towards uptake of healthy habits for better living. Don't listen to us, your body will feel the benefits soon enough!

EXAMPLES OF WEIGHT WATCHERS ZERO POINTS FOOD LIST:

- Apples
- Applesauce, unsweetened
- Artichokes
- Arugula
- Asparagus
- Apricots
- Arrowroot
- Artichoke hearts
- Bamboo shoots
- Banana

- Beans: cannellini, cranberry (Roman), green, garbanzo (chickpeas), kidney,

- lima, lupini, mung, navy, pink, pinto, small white, snap, soy, string, wax, white
- Beans, refried, fat-free, canned
- Broccoli slaw
- Broccolini
- Brussels sprouts
- Blackberries
- Blueberries
- Broccoli
- Broccoli rabe
- Beets
- Berries, mixed

- Cabbage: all varieties including bok choy, Japanese, green, red, napa, savory, pickled
- Cauliflower
- Caviar
- Celery
- Calamari, grilled
- Cantaloupe
- Carrots
- Swiss chard
- Cherries
- Chicken breast, ground chicken
- Chicken breast or tenderloin, skinless, boneless or with bone
- Clementines
- Coleslaw mix
- Collards
- Daikon
- Dates, fresh
- Eggplant
- Eggs, whole, including yolks
- Endive
- Escarole
- Dragon fruit
- Corn, baby corn
- Cranberries
- Cucumber
- Edamame, in pods or shelled
- Egg substitutes
- Egg whites
- Figs

- Fish: Almost all kind of fish

- Garlic
- Ginger root
- Grapefruit
- Grapes
- Greens: beet, collard, dandelion, kale, mustard, turnip
- Greens, mixed baby
- Guavas
- Guavas, strawberry

- Hearts of palm (palmetto)
- Honeydew melon
- Jackfruit
- Jerk chicken breast
- Artichokes

- Kiwifruit
- Kumquats
- Lime zest
- Lychees
- Mangoes
- Melon balls
- Mung bean sprouts
- Leeks
- Lemon
- Lemon zest
- Lentils
- Lettuce

- Lime
- Mung dal
- Mushroom caps
- Mushrooms: all kinds
- Nectarine
- Nori seaweed

- Peas and carrots
- Peas:all kinds
- Peppers, all varieties
- Pepperoncini
- Onions
- Oranges
- Papayas
- Parsley
- Passion fruit
- Pea shoots
- Peaches
- Peapods, black-eye
- Pears

- Persimmons
- Pickles, unsweetened
- Pico de gallo
- Pimientos, canned
- Pineapple
- Plums
- Pomegranate seeds
- Pomegranates

- Pumpkin
- Pumpkin puree
- Radicchio
- Radishes
- Raspberries
- Rutabagas

- Salad, mixed greens
- Salad, three-bean
- Salad, tossed, without dressing
- Salsa verde
- Salsa, fat free
- Salsa, fat free; gluten-free
- Sashimi
- Satay, chicken, without peanut sauce
- Satsuma mandarin
- Sauerkraut
- Scallions
- Seaweed
- Shallots

- Shellfish: abalone, clams, crab (including Alaska king, blue, dungeness, lump crabmeat, queen) crayfish, cuttlefish, lobster (including

- spiny lobster), mussels, octopus, oysters, scallops, shrimp, squid
- Spinach
- Sprouts, including alfalfa, bean, lentil
- Strawberries
- Succotash

- Tangelo
- Tangerine
- Taro
- Tofu, all varieties
- Tofu, smoked
- Tomatillos
- Tomato puree
- Tomato sauce
- Tomatoes: all varieties including plum, grape, cherry
- Turkey breast, ground, 99% fat-free
- Turkey breast or tenderloin, skinless, boneless or with bone
- Turkey breast, skinless, smoked
- Turnips

- Vegetable sticks
- Vegetables, mixed
- Vegetables, stir fry, without sauce

- Water chestnuts
- Watercress
- Watermelon

- Yogurt, Greek, plain, nonfat, unsweetened
- Yogurt, plain, nonfat, unsweetened
- Yogurt, soy, plain

Limit these Food In Your Diet

- Sugar is a cause of many diseases like diabetes and other heart ailments. Artificial sweeteners are also not a very healthy option even though they don't have calories.

- Grains can be quite fattening especially gluten grains like wheat and barley. Rice and oats are a healthier alternative.

- Trans fat-containing foods are unhealthy and found in many processed foods.

- Foods labeled as "diet" or "low-fat" are not healthy either. They usually contain a lot of sugar and are quite processed.

- Processed foods, in general, are not a very healthy option. They contain harmful additives and have low nutritive value as well.

- Alcohol is also harmful to your body in general and can cause weight gain if excessively consumed in forms like beer. A glass of wine or two is not as harmful.
- Sodas and other sugary drinks actually contain a lot of sugar and many chemicals as well.

- Deep-fried food like chips and French fries are also bad for your body and contain a lot of calories.

- Ice cream and chocolates should be consumed in a controlled amount and not too frequently.

We don't recommend that you completely cut off these foods from your diet. If you especially like a certain food, it is even harder to stick to a diet that restricts you from having that food completely. This is why you should just be more conscious about how much you eat these foods without having to feel guilty about it later. As you become more conscious about what you eat, it will become a more natural initiative for you to choose the healthier option the next time you eat.

Include These Food In Your Diet:

- Eggs are a very nutritious option for you as long as you do not consume too many

- Meat is a healthy addition to your diet too. Please includes meat whenever possible. Fresh Lean Meat (Any kind is the way to go)

- Fish is one of the healthiest things to include in your diet. Fish contains many nutrients and healthy omega-3 fatty acids, it help your brain to work properly.

- Fruits (all kinds) should be included in your diet regularly ,they contains vitamin C which also one of the most important thing that our body need everyday.

- Vegetables is a must to includes in your daily meals, they provide your body lots of nutrients , if you want to gain the maximum benefits in your well-being

- Nuts and seeds , contains a lot of Vitamin E, but they're should be consumed in moderation because of their high-calorie content.

Carbohydrates : Even though when you are a diet, too much Carbs is not good, but they are still should be consumed in moderation but not completely restricted even if you are trying to lose weight. Once you are more aware of how different foods affect your body, you can make better choices. Healthy eating habits to incorporate into your daily life:

- Drink water. Cut out the habits of drinking alcohol or other sweet drinks, by introduce water intake more often and make as a routine of Drinking a glass of warm water with honey and lemon juice after you wake up every day, will do you even better

- Pay attention to your serving sizes during meals, especially the grains. Split dishes with a friend when you eat out. Avoid ordering large portions of anything because your body does not need it.

- Eat slowly and chew well after each bite in order to help digest your food well. Your brain then processes when you have had enough food. This does not happen on time when you gulp down food too fast.

- Eat a filling breakfast every single day without skipping.

- Eat small meals throughout the day instead of three large meals. This keeps your energy level up the whole day and also prevents binge eating due to hunger.

- Choose healthier cooking methods like grilling. When you stir fry your meat or veggies, use a few healthy oils like olive oil. Steaming vegetables is also good. Replace salt with herbs or spices.

- Eat dinner at least a couple of hours before you sleep.

- Do not eat large snacks after dinner.

- Include fiber in your meals in the form of whole grains, apple, berries, beans, vegetables, etc.

- Limit your salt intake. Keep note of the content especially in packaged foods, as they tend to be high in salt..

- Eat the actual fruit instead of opting for juices, especially processed juices. The fruit will benefit your body much more. They give you more fiber

- Choose lean meat and cut down on animal fat in your diet. Animal fat will increase bad cholesterol levels in your body.

- Consume calcium and vitamin D in your diet for bone health.
- Avoid alcohol or limit it to a glass or two a day if you must. Moderate amounts of wine or such might benefit you but the problems associated with too much alcohol suggest you avoid it altogether.

WW FREESTYLE RECIPES

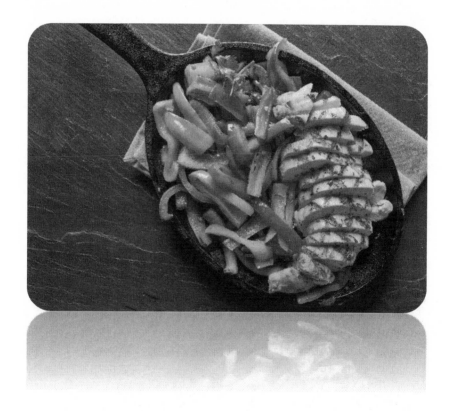

Mushroom Ginger Chicken Soup

Serves: 5 servings

Serving size: 1 cup

Freestyle SmartPoints: 0

Ingredients

- 1 pound boneless, skinless chicken breast
- 8 ounces fresh mushrooms
- 2 tablespoons lemon juice
- 1 teaspoon garlic, minced
- 1 teaspoon fresh ginger, ground
- 2 cups fat-free chicken broth
- 2 tablespoons reduced-sodium soy
- 3 scallions, thinly sliced
- 1 leek

Instructions

Cook the chicken, mushrooms, lemon juice, garlic and ginger in a medium saucepan over medium heat about 5 minutes.

You may recognize this next step (the leek) from our Creamy Chicken and Stuffing Casserole. (I hope we can all agree that leeks are cool at this point, and totally worth including in this healthy soup).

Meanwhile, cut the top of the leek off (the darkest green part). You will not be using the top half so that part can be discarded.

Slice into the bottom portion of the leek going lengthwise starting about 1-2 inches from the bottom of the leek.

Rotate the leek and slice it the lengthwise again. Do this a couple of more times until you have very thin sliced strips

Now chop the leek into small pieces starting from the top.Rinse the small pieces of the leek.

Add broth, soy sauce, scallions and leek and cook for 7-8 more minutes.

Nutrition Information

Calories: 169

Fat: 3 g

Saturated fat: 1 g

Trans fat: 0 g

Carbohydrates: 3 g

Sugar: 0 g

Sodium: 490 mg

Fiber: 1 g

Protein: 22 g

Cholesterol: 68 mg

Turkey Meatball & Veggie

Serve: 8

Free style Smart point: 5

Ingredients:

- Cooking spray
- 1 onion, chopped
- 3-4 carrots, sliced or chopped
- 1 cup green beans, cut
- 2 minced garlic cloves
- 1 (24 ounce) package Jennie-O Italian style turkey meatballs
- 2 (14.5 ounce) cans beef or vegetable broth
- 2 (14.5 ounce) diced or Italian stewed tomatoes
- 1-1/2 cups frozen corn
- 1 teaspoon oregano
- 1 teaspoon parsley
- ½ teaspoon basil

Instructions:

1. Spray large saucepan or instant pot with cooking spray.
2. Add onions, carrots, green beans and garlic and cook over medium heat 2-3 minutes.
3. Mix in remaining ingredients.

4. If cooking on a stovetop, cover and cook over medium-low heat for 20 minutes, or until meatballs are heated through.

5. -OR-

6. If using an instant pot, press the "soup" button and cook on high pressure for 15 minutes. Vent to release pressure once cooked.

7. -OR-

8. Cook in a slow cooker for 5-6 hours on LOW.

9. Serve warm.

10. Refrigerate or freeze leftovers.

Nutrition Information

- **Calories: 285**
- **Fat: 13 g**
- **Saturated fat: 4 g**
- **Trans fat: 0 g**
- **Carbohydrates: 21 g**
- **Sugar: 9 g**
- **Sodium: 1126 mg**
- **Fiber: 3 g**
- **Protein: 19 g**

Balsamic Chicken Lettuce Wraps

Freestyle SmartPoints: 1
Makes 12 servings

Ingredients

- 2 T. lemon juice
- ¼ c. balsamic vinegar
- 2 T. red wine vinegar
- 1 T. honey
- 2 T. water
- 1 t. dried oregano
- ½ t. onion powder
- ½ t. garlic powder
- 1 lb. boneless, skinless chicken breasts
- 1 medium zucchini
- 1 medium red bell pepper
- ½ c. diced red onion
- 8 grape tomatoes
- ½ c. chickpeas
- ½ c. feta cheese
- 1 large head iceberg lettuce
- ⅓ c. plain nonfat Greek yogurt, optional
- Fresh parsley

Instructions

In a small bowl mix the lemon juice, balsamic vinegar, red wine vinegar, honey, water, oregano, onion powder, and garlic powder. In a large sauté pan coated with cooking spray cook the chicken over medium-high heat until it begins to turn white on the outside (about 2 minutes) and add ½ of the vinaigrette to the pan.

Continue to cook until the chicken is cooked through (about 5 additional minutes) and the vinaigrette has evaporated. Remove the pan from the heat and pour the chicken in to a large bowl. If you prefer the zucchini, bell peppers, and red onions to be cooked, add them to the saute pan and cook for 2 to 4 minute, or until zucchini becomes soft and the onions become translucent.

In a medium bowl combine the zucchini, bell peppers, onions, tomatoes, chickpeas, and feta with the remaining vinaigrette and stir to combine.

Add the toppings to the cooked chicken and stir to combine. Add the toppings to the cooked chicken and stir to combine. Toss salad with yogurt and parsley just before serving if desired.To make the lettuce wraps, cut off the stem of the lettuce head and cut in half lengthwise. Peel off individual leaves and wash and pat dry.

Scoop ½ cup of the mixture in each lettuce wrap and top with a dollop of yogurt and fresh parsley if desired.

One Pot Butter Chicken Pasta

Free Style Smart Point: 2

Yield: 8 (1 1/4 CUPS) Serving

Ingredients:

- 1 ½ lbs uncooked boneless, skinless chicken breasts
- 4 tablespoons light butter
- ½ cup chopped onion
- ¼ cup flour
- ½ teaspoon salt
- ¼ teaspoon black pepper
- 1 ½ cups skim milk
- 2 ½ cups water*
- 1 tablespoon Better Than Bouillon Roasted Chicken Base
- ½ teaspoon poultry seasoning
- 8 oz uncooked egg noodles
- 1 cup frozen corn kernels
- 2 cups frozen peas and carrots

Instructions:

1. Place the chicken breasts in a Dutch oven or other large pot and cover with water to about 2 inches over the chicken.

2. Bring the water to a boil over high heat and then reduce the heat to medium. Cook over medium heat for 15-20 minutes (depending on the thickness of your

chicken breasts – mine are generally done at 15, so check one then) until chicken is cooked through.

3.   Remove the chicken breasts to a cutting board. Discard the water from the pot and rinse and wipe out the pot to use again. Chop the chicken into small, bite-size pieces and set aside.

4.   Melt the butter in the pot over medium heat. Add the chopped onion and cook for a few minutes until the onion is softened.

5.   Whisk in the flour, salt and pepper until combined with the butter and onions and continue to whisk for another 1-2 minutes.

6.   Slowly whisk in the milk until combined and smooth. Add the water and bouillon base (or broth) and poultry seasoning and whisk in to combine.

7.   Increase the heat to med-high and stir occasionally until boiling. Reduce the heat to med-low and add the egg noodles. Cook for 8 minutes, stirring regularly to prevent sticking. If you need a little more liquid toward the end you can add a bit more water or broth. Add the chopped chicken, corn, and peas and carrots and stir until thoroughly combined. Cook for another few minutes until all ingredients are heated through.

Nutrition Information:

314 calories,

35 g carbs,

2 g saturated fat,

27 g protein,

3 g fiber

Delight Slow Cooker Chicken

Freestyle SmartPoints: 0

Ingredients:

- 8 chicken breast
- 3/4 teaspoon kosher salt
- freshly ground black pepper
- cooking spray
- 5 garlic cloves, finely chopped
- 1/2 large onion, chopped
- 1 28-ounce can crushed tomatoes
- 1/2 medium red bell pepper, chopped
- 1/2 medium green bell pepper, chopped
- 4 ounce sliced shiitake mushrooms
- 1 sprig of fresh thyme
- 1 sprig of fresh oregano
- 1 bay leaf
- 1 tablespoon chopped fresh parsley
- 1 grated Parmesan cheese, for serving (optional)

Instsructions:

Season the chicken with salt and pepper to taste. Heat a large nonstick skillet over medium-high heat. Coat with cooking spray, add the chicken, and cook until browned- 2 to 3 minutes per side. Transfer to your slow cooker.

Reduce the heat under the skillet to medium and coat with more cooking spray. Add the garlic and onion and cook, stirring, until soft- 3 to 4 minutes. Transfer to the slow cooker and add the tomatoes, bell peppers, mushrooms, thyme, oregano and bay leaf. Stir to combine.

Cover and cook on high for 4 hours or on low for 8 hours.

Discard the bay leaf and transfer the chicken to a large plate. Pull the chicken meat from the bones shred the meat, and return it to the sauce. Stir in the parsley . If desired, serve topped with Parmesan cheese.

Nutritional information :

Calories: 220,

Fat: 6g,

Sat Fat: 1.5g,

Cholesterol: 123mg,

Sodium: 319mg,

Carbohydrates: 10g,

Fiber: 2g,

Sugar: 6g,

Protein: 31g

Healthy Vegetarian Chili

Makes 8: 1 cup/servings

Freestyle SmartPoints: 1

Ingredients:

- 2 cans (15 oz. each) kidney beans
- 1 can (8 oz.) tomato sauce
- 1 can (14.5 oz.) diced tomatoes
- 1 packet (1 oz.) chili seasoning mix
- 1 pkg. (13.5 oz.) Gardein Beefless Ground

Instructions:

Mix kidney beans, tomato sauce, diced tomatoes, and chili seasoning in a large stockpot. Allow to cook on medium heat for 5-7 minutes.

Add the beefless ground and cook an additional 5 minutes, or until heated through.Top with whatever you like.

Nutrition Information:

Calories: 153

Fat: 2 g

Saturated fat: 0 g

Sugar: 4 g

Sodium: 561 mg

Fiber: 7 g

Protein: 14 g

Cholesterol: 0 mg

Cumin Grilled Shrimp Kebabs

Serve: 8

Serving Size: 1 kebab

Freestyle SmartPoints: 0

Ingredients:

- 32 jumbo raw shrimp, peeled and deveined3 cloves garlic, crushed
- 24 slices (about 3) large limes, very thinly sliced into rounds (optional)
- olive oil cooking spray
- 1 tsp kosher salt
- 1 1/2 tsp ground cumin
- 1/4 cup chopped fresh cilantro, divided
- 16 bamboo skewers soaked in water 1 hour
- 1 lime cut into 8 wedges

Instructions:

Heat the grill on medium heat and spray the grates with oil.

Season the shrimp with garlic, cumin, salt and half of the cilantro in a medium bowl.

Beginning and ending with shrimp, thread the shrimp and folded lime slices onto 8 pairs of parallel skewers to make 8 kebabs total.

Grill the shrimp, turning occasionally, until shrimp is opaque throughout, about 1 to 2 minutes on each side.

Top with remaining cilantro and fresh squeezed lime juice before serving.

Nutrition Information

Calories: 74

Total Fat: 1g

Saturated Fat: g

Cholesterol: 94mg

Sodium: 384mg

Carbohydrates: 3g

Fiber: 1g

Sugar: 0g

Protein: 13g

Garlic White Chicken Chili

Free Style Smart Points: 2
Yield: 8 (1 Cup) Serving

Ingredients:

* 1 tablespoon Canola oil
* 2 cups yellow onion, chopped
* 2 tablespoons chili powder
* 1 tablespoon minced garlic
* 2 teaspoons ground cumin
* 1 teaspoon oregano
* 3 (15.5 oz.) cans Great Northern beans, rinsed and drained
* 4 cups reduced sodium fat free chicken broth
* 3 cups chopped or shredded cooked skinless chicken breast
* 1 (14.5 oz) can diced tomatoes
* 1/3 cup chopped fresh cilantro
* 2 tablespoon fresh lime juice
* ½ teaspoon salt
* ½ teaspoon pepper

Instructions:

1.	Bring oil to medium heat in a large pot or Dutch oven. Add the onions and sauté for 5-8 minutes or until tender.

2.	Add the chili powder, garlic and cumin and stir to coat the onions. Cook for 2 more minutes. Add the oregano and beans, stir and cook for 30 more seconds.

3.	Add the broth and reduce the heat to medium-low. Simmer for 20 minutes, stirring occasionally.

4.	Remove 2 cups of the bean/broth mixture into a blender (or container for an immersion blender) and process until smooth.

5.	Return pureed mixture to the pot. Add the chicken and tomatoes and cook over medium-low for another 30 minutes, stirring occasionally.

6.	Add the cilantro, lime juice, salt & pepper and stir to combine before serving.

Nutrition Information:

291 calories,

36 g carbs,

4 g sugars,

4 g fat,

1 g saturated fat,

27 g protein,

12 g fiber

Add the asparagus and garlic to the skillet and cook for 2-3 minutes, stirring often

Add the chicken broth and vinegar to the skillet. Stir and scrape any browned bits off the bottom of the pan. Add the chicken and let simmer for 5-10 minutes on low heat or until chicken is fully cooked. Squeeze the rest lemon juice over top.

Nutritional Information:

Calories 239

Total Fat 5g

Saturated Fat 1g

Cholesterol 0mg

Dietary Fiber 2g

9%

Sugars 2g

Protein 38g

Ginger Coconut Chicken Skewers

Serving: 4

Freestyle SmartPoints: 1

Ingredients:

- ¼ cup low sodium soy sauce
- 2 oz canned pineapple juice
- ¼ cup light coconut milk
- 2 tablespoons honey
- 2 garlic cloves, minced
- 1 tablespoon grated ginger
- ½ teaspoon sesame oil
- 2 scallions, chopped
- 1 lb fresh pineapple, cut into bite-sized pieces
- 1 ½ pounds (24 oz) raw boneless, skinless chicken breasts, cut into bite sized chunks
- You'll also need 12" skewers

Instructions:

To create the marinade, combine the soy sauce, pineapple juice, coconut milk, honey, garlic, ginger, sesame oil, and scallions and mix thoroughly.

Pour marinade into a gallon Ziploc bag and add chicken. Seal bag and shake to coat chicken in the marinade.

Place the bag in the refrigerator so that the chicken is covered in the marinade and refrigerate for at least 4 hours .

Pre-heat the grill until hot. Divide the chicken and pineapple evenly onto the eight skewers.

Place the skewers directly on the grill or a skewer rack over the grill over low heat.

Cooking yours for about 5-6 minutes and then flipping them and continuing to cook until chicken is cooked through.

Nutrition Information:

220 calories,

6 g carbs,

4 g fat,

41 g protein,

1 g fiber

Parsley Egg Noodles Chicken Soup

Serve: 10

Serving Size: 1.5 cups

Freestyle SmartPoints: 2

Ingredients:

- 1 lb. boneless, skinless chicken breast
- 1/2 tsp. pepper
- 1 medium onion, chopped
- 1 tbsp. EVOO
- 6 garlic cloves, minced
- 3 celery ribs, sliced
- 3 medium carrots, sliced
- 2 tbsp. dried parsley flakes
- 4 tsp. Italian seasoning
- 12 cups fat-free chicken broth
- 3-1/2 cups uncooked egg noodles

Instructions:

Heat oil in a large stockpot. Saute onion, celery, and carrots in oil until onion is tender.

Add garlic and cook one minute longer.

Add the chicken broth, chicken, parsley, Italian seasoning. Bring to a boil. Reduce heat; cover and simmer for 20 minutes.

Stir in noodles. Return to a boil and cook 7-9 more minutes, or until the noodles are soft.Add salt and pepper to taste.

Instant Pot Grapefruit Juice Cuban Pork

Free Style Smart Points: 5
Yield: 10 servings, Serving Size: a little over 3 oz.

Ingredients:

- 3 lb. boneless pork shoulder blade roast, lean, all fat removed
- 6 cloves garlic
- juice of 1 grapefruit (about 2/3 cup)
- juice of 1 lime
- 1/2 tablespoon fresh oregano
- 1/2 tablespoon cumin
- 1 tablespoon kosher salt
- 1 bay leaf
- lime wedges, for serving
- chopped cilantro, for serving
- hot sauce, for serving
- tortillas, optional for serving
- salsa, optional for serving

Instructions:

1. Cut the pork in 4 pieces and place in a bowl.
2. In a small blender or mini food processor, combine garlic, grapefruit juice, lime juice, oregano, cumin and salt and blend until smooth.

3.   Pour the marinade over the pork and let it sit room temperature 1 hour or refrigerated as long as overnight.

4.   Transfer to the pressure cooker, add the bay leaf, cover and cook high pressure 80 minutes. Let the pressure release naturally.

5.   Remove pork and shred using two forks.

6.   Remove liquid from pressure cooker, reserving then place the pork back into pressure cooker. Add about 1 cup of the liquid (jus) back, adjust the salt as needed and keep warm until you're ready to eat.

Nutrition Information:
- Calories: 213
- Total Fat: 9.5g
- Saturated Fat: 0g
- Sodium: 440.5mg
- Carbohydrates: 2.5g
- Fiber: 0.5g
- Sugar: 1.5g
- Protein: 26.5g

Mozzarella Cheese Spinach manicotti

Yield: 8 servings, Serving Size: 2 manicotti
Free Style Smart Points: 5

Ingredients:
- 16 homemade crespelles
- 15 oz. part skim ricotta cheese (I use Polly-O)
- 2 cups shredded part-skim mozzarella cheese (reserve 1/2 cup) Polly-O
- 1 large egg
- 10 oz. package frozen spinach, thawed and squeezed really well
- 1/4 cup grated Parmesan Regianno
- 1/2 teaspoon kosher salt
- black pepper, to taste
- 2 1/2 cups jarred marinara

Instructions:
1. Start by making the crespelles.
2. Preheat oven to 375°F.
3. In a large bowl, combine ricotta, 1-1/2 cups of the mozzarella, egg, spinach, parmesan cheese, 1/2 teaspoon salt and pepper.
4. Fill each crespelle with 1/4 cup spinach filling and roll.

5.　　In a large baking dish, (or two smaller dishes) pour 1 cup of sauce on the bottom of the dish.

6.　　Place rolled manicotti seem side down onto baking dish. Top with 1 1/2 cups more sauce and remaining mozzarella cheese.

7.　　Cover with foil and bake about about 25 minutes, until hot and bubbling, and the cheese is melted.

Nutrition Information:
- Calories: 277
- Total Fat: 12.5g
- Saturated Fat: 6g
- Sodium: 698mg
- Carbohydrates: 20g
- Fiber: 3g
- Sugar: 5g
- Protein: 22.5g

Garlic Beans Chili Chicken

Yield: 8 (1 cup) servings

Freestyle SmartPoints: 1

Ingredients:

- 1 tablespoon Canola oil
- 2 cups yellow onion, chopped
- 2 tablespoons chili powder
- 1 tablespoon minced garlic
- 2 teaspoons ground cumin
- 1 teaspoon oregano
- 3 (15.5 oz.) cans Great Northern beans, rinsed and drained
- 4 cups reduced sodium fat free chicken broth
- 3 cups chopped or shredded cooked skinless chicken breast
- 1 (14.5 oz) can diced tomatoes
- 1/3 cup chopped fresh cilantro
- 2 tablespoon fresh lime juice
- ½ teaspoon salt
- ½ teaspoon pepper

Instructions:

Bring oil to medium heat in a large pot or Dutch oven. Add the onions and sauté for 5-8 minutes or until tender. Add the chili powder, garlic and cumin and stir to coat the onions.

Cook for 2 more minutes. Add the oregano and beans, stir and cook for 30 more seconds. Add the broth and reduce the heat to medium-low. Simmer for 20 minutes, stirring occasionally.

Remove 2 cups of the bean/broth mixture into a blender and process until smooth. Return pureed mixture to the pot. Add the chicken and tomatoes and cook over medium-low for another 30 minutes, stirring occasionally. Add the cilantro, lime juice, salt & pepper and stir to combine before serving.

Nutrition Information:

291 calories,

36 g carbs,

4 g sugars,

4 g fat,

1 g saturated fat,

27 g protein,

12 g fiber

2.   In a large saute pan or walled skillet, bring the olive oil over medium heat. Add the chicken in a single layer and cook on one side for 3-4 minutes.

3.   Flip each piece and cook for an additional 3 minutes or until each piece is cooked through. Transfer the chicken to a side plate and cover with aluminum foil to keep warm.

4.   Add the cauliflower rice, salsa, water, the remaining tablespoon of taco seasoning, corn and black beans to the skillet and stir to combine.

5.   Cover and cook over medium for 5 minutes. Remove the lid to stir, cover and reduce heat to medium-low. Continue to cook for another 5 minutes or until the cauliflower is softened.

6.   Remove the lid, stir the contents and then sprinkle the cheese over the top. Add the reserved chicken in a single layer on top of the cheese and replace the lid.

7.   Turn off the burner and let the skillet sit, covered, for 1-2 minutes until the cheese is melted.

Nutrition Information:

316 calories,

23 g carbs,

4 g sugars,

3 g saturated fat,

35 g protein,

5 g fiber

Spicy Onion Salsa Roasted Salmon

Serving size: 1 fillet with salsa

Freestyle SmartPoints: 0

Ingredients:

- 1 medium plum tomato, roughly chopped
- 1/2 small onion, roughly chopped
- 1 clove garlic, minced
- 1 small jalapeño pepper, seeded and roughly chopped
- 1 teaspoon cider vinegar
- 1/2 teaspoon chili powder
- 1/4 teaspoon ground cumin
- 1/4 teaspoon salt
- 2 to 3 dashes hot sauce
- Two 4-ounce salmon fillets

Instructions:

Preheat oven to 400°F.

Place tomato, onion, garlic, jalapeño, vinegar, chili powder, cumin, salt and hot sauce in a food processor; process until finely chopped and uniform.

Place salmon in a medium roasting pan; spoon the salsa on top. Roast until the salmon is just cooked through, 12 to 15 minutes.

Nutritional Information:

Calories: 211,

Fat: 10g,

Saturated Fat: 1.75g,

Sugar: 1.87g,

Fiber: 1.10g,

Protein: 25g,

Cholesterol: 70.3mg,

Carbohydrates: 4.5g

Delight Turkey Chili

Freestyle SmartPoints: 1

Serves: 8

Ingredients

- 2 cups shredded cooked turkey
- ½ cup diced onion
- ½ green pepper, diced
- ½ cup diced celery
- 2 tablespoons olive oil
- 1 tablespoon minced garlic
- 2 cups chicken broth
- 3 cans (15-16 oz) white beans / great northern beans
- ¼ teaspoon cayenne pepper
- 1 teaspoon ground cumin
- ¾ teaspoon oregano
- ½ teaspoon salt
- ¼ teaspoon ground black pepper
- shredded Parmesan cheese, sour cream, and cilantro for serving if desired

Instructions:

In a large stock pot or dutch oven, add onion, green pepper, celery and olive oil. Cook on medium-high heat until onions are translucent and peppers are tender. Stir in garlic.

Add chicken broth, beans, and turkey and mix well. Stir in seasonings. Heat to boiling then reduce heat to simmer and cover for 30-60 minutes, stirring occasionally.

Heat to boiling then reduce heat to simmer and cover for 30-60 minutes, stirring occasionally.

Serve with sour cream, cheese, and cilantro.

Nutritional Information

Calories: 460,

Fat: 5.6g,

Saturated Fat: 1.1g, S

ugar: 2.5g,

Fiber: 19g,

Cholesterol: 64mg,

Caramelized Paprika Pork Chops

Serve: 6

Free Style Smartpoints: 3

Ingredients

- ½ lbs. Lean pork chops, fat removed
- 2-3 Tbsp. Soy sauce
- 1-2 tsp. Paprika
- 1 large or 2 small onions
- Cooking spray

Instructions

Preheat the grill pan Be sure to trim off the fat from the pork chops, if there is any.

Sprinkle the pork chops with paprika.

Spray the grill pan with cooking spray. Set pork chops on the grill. Pour soy sauce over the pork.

Flip the pork chops over. Cover the chops with the grill press, if you have one. Cook five minutes.

While pork chops are cooking, slice onions. I slice mine kind of thick.

Flip the pork chops over again and allow to cook for another five minutes. Once fully cooked, transfer pork chops to a plate.

Cook onion on the grill pan for about 5 minutes, or until slightly softened and caramelized. The onions will pick up the flavor from the pork chops.

Serve and enjoy

Tasty Chicken Nuggets

Serve: 8

Free Style Smartpoint: 2

Ingredients:

2 lbs. boneless skinless chicken

½ cup ketchup

⅓ cup brewed coffee

¼ cup packed brown sugar

⅛ cup apple-cider vinegar

1 garlic clove, minced

½ tsp. salt

⅛ tsp. red pepper flakes

Instructions

Spray grill pan with nonstick spray. Preheat grill to medium or medium-high heat.

Cut chicken into small pieces.

Combine ketchup, coffee, brown sugar, vinegar, garlic, ¼ tsp. salt, and pepper flakes in medium saucepan and set over medium heat. Cook, stirring, until mixture comes to a boil.

Reduce heat and simmer 10 minutes.

Meanwhile, Sprinkle chicken with remaining ¼ teaspoon salt. Place chicken on grill pan and allow to cook, turning occasionally, 10-15 minutes.

Brush chicken with sauce, and grill until instant-read thermometer inserted in center registers 165 degrees and the sauce begins to carmelize on the chicken, about 5-10 minutes longer.

Nutrition Information:

Calories: 234

Fat: 4 g

Saturated fat: 0 g

Sugar: 7 g

Sodium: 243 mg

Fiber: 0 g

Protein: 24 g

Cholesterol: 92 mg

Spinach Ham Egg Cups

Yield: 12 egg cups

Free Style Smart Points: 1

Ingredients:

- 9 oz thinly sliced deli ham, divided (I used Hillshire Farm Deli Select)
- 6 large eggs
- 2 egg whites
- ¼ cup skim milk
- ¼ teaspoon salt
- 1/8 teaspoon pepper
- ½ cup chopped fresh spinach leaves
- 2 oz shredded 2% sharp cheddar cheese, divided

Instructions:

1. Preheat the oven to 350. Lightly mist 12 cups in a muffin tin with cooking spray. Press a slice of ham into each cup of the muffin tin, arranging the edges to form a ham cup.

2. Chop up the remaining ham (my slices were about ½ ounce each so I had around 3 ounces remaining) and set aside.

3. In a mixing bowl, combine the eggs, egg whites, milk, salt and pepper and whisk together until yolks and whites are fully combined and beaten.

4.   Add the reserved chopped ham, the spinach and half of the shredded cheddar and stir together to combine.

5.   Spoon the egg mixture evenly into the ham cups and then top each cup with the remaining shredded cheese. Place the tin in the oven and bake for 18-20 minutes until the eggs are set.

Nutrition Information:

82 calories,

2 g carbs,

1 g sugars,

4 g fat,

2 g saturated fat,

9 g protein,

0 g fiber

Cheesy Chives Zucchini Corn Frittata

Free Style Smart Points: 2
Yield: 6 SLICES

Ingredients:

- 1 medium ear of fresh raw corn
- 1 tablespoon light butter
- 1 cup thin sliced zucchini
- 8 large eggs
- 1/3 cup 2% plain Greek yogurt
- ¾ teaspoon salt (plus a sprinkle more for the corn & zucchini)
- ¼ teaspoon black pepper (plus a sprinkle more for the corn & zucchini)
- 1 tablespoon diced chives
- ¼ cup sliced fresh basil
- 2 oz sharp cheddar cheese, shredded

Instructions:

1. Pre-heat your oven to 350. Shuck the corn and remove any remaining strings. Use a large sharp knife to cut off the kernels as close to the cob as you can get (I ended up with about 1 cup of kernels).

2.   Melt the butter in an 8"-10" oven-safe nonstick deep skillet over medium-low heat. Add the corn kernels and the sliced zucchini and stir to coat.

3.   Sprinkle with a bit of salt and pepper to taste. Cook, stirring regularly, for 6-8 minutes or until corn and zucchini are cooked through.

4.   While the corn and zucchini are cooking, break the eggs into a large mixing bowl and whisk together until just combined.

5.   Add the yogurt, salt, black pepper, chives, basil and shredded cheese and stir together until mixed.

6.   When the corn and zucchini are cooked, transfer them into the bowl containing the egg mixture and stir together. Spray the skillet you used liberally with cooking spray and then pour the egg mixture into the skillet.

7.   Cook on a burner set to medium heat for 5-7 minutes until the very outside edge of the frittata starts to turn opaque/look cooked.

8.   Transfer the skillet into the oven and cook for 15-17 minutes until the center is set. Let cool for 5 minutes, then slice into 6 slices and serve.

Nutrition Information:

167 calories,

5 g carbs,

2 g sugars,

5 g saturated fat,

13 g protein,

1 g fiber

Yummy Buffalo Chicken

Yield: 12 (1/2 cup) servings

Freestyle SmartPoints: 1

Ingredients:

- 3 lbs raw boneless skinless chicken breasts
- 12 oz bottle of Buffalo wing sauce
- 1 oz packet of dry Ranch mix
- 2 tablespoons light butter

Instructions

Place the chicken breasts in your slow cooker. Pour the bottle of wing sauce over the top of the chicken. Sprinkle the packet of ranch mix over the top of the wing sauce. Place the lid on your slow cooker. Cook on low for 7-9 hours until meat shreds easily.

Remove meat and shred it using two forks. Return shredded meat to the sauce and add the butter. Stir to combine. Continue to cook on low for another hour so the meat can soak up the sauce. Serve however you like!

Nutrition Information:

175 calories, 1 g carbs, 0 g sugars, 5 g fat, 1 g saturated fat, 28 g protein, 0 g fiber

Quick N' Easy Sandwiches

Serve: 5 Sandwiches

Free Style Smartpoints: 3

Ingredients:

- 6 hard-boiled eggs
- 2 tablespoons tarter sauce
- 1 tablespoon mustard
- 1 teaspoon sugar
- 10 slices light bread

Instructions

Chop up the hard-boiled eggs.

Mix tarter sauce, mustard, and sugar into the eggs.

Scoop ¼ cup egg salad mixture onto 5 pieces of bread and top each with another piece of bread. Cut sandwiches in half.

Nutrition Information:

Calories: 169

Fat: 8 g

Saturated fat: 0 g

Sugar: 3 g

Sodium: 344 mg

Fiber: 4 g

Protein: 13 g

Cholesterol: 198 mg

Thyme Tenderloin Ragu

Serve:10

Free Style Smarpoint: 1

Ingredients:

- 18 oz pork tenderloin
- 1 teaspoon kosher salt
- black pepper, to taste
- 1 tsp olive oil
- 5 cloves garlic, smashed with the side of a knife
- 1 (28 oz can) crushed tomatoes
- 1 small jar roasted red peppers, drained
- 2 sprigs fresh thyme
- 2 bay leaves
- 1 tbsp chopped fresh parsley, divided

Instructions:

Season pork with salt and pepper. Heat a large pot or Dutch oven over medium-high heat, add oil and garlic and saute until golden brown, 1 to 1 1/2 minutes;

Remove with a slotted spoon. Add pork and brown about 2 minutes on each side. Add the remaining ingredients to the pot including the garlic, reserving half of the parsley.

Bring to a boil, cook covered on low until the pork is tender, and shreds easily, about 2 hours. Remove bay leaves, shred the pork with 2 forks and top with remaining parsley. Serve over your favorite pasta.

Nutrition Information:

Calories: 93

Total Fat: 1.5g

Saturated Fat: g

Cholesterol: 33mg

Sodium: 347mg

Carbohydrates: 6.5g

Fiber: 0g

Sugar: 3g

Protein: 11g

Greek-Style Chickpea Salad

Free Style Smart Points: 0
Serve: 8

Ingredients:

- 2 (15 ounce) cans chickpea, drained and rinsed
- 1 small tomato, chopped
- ¼ cup finely chopped red onion
- ½ teaspoon sugar
- ¼ cup reduced fat crumbled feta cheese
- ½ tablespoon lemon juice
- ½ tablespoon red wine vinegar
- 1 tablespoon plain nonfat Greek Yogurt
- 2 cloves garlic, minced
- ¼ teaspoon salt
- ¼ teaspoon pepper
- 1-2 tablespoons cilantro

Instructions:

1. Drain and rinse the chickpeas and place in a medium bowl.
2. Toss in the rest of the ingredients until chickpeas are evenly coated and all of the ingredients are mixed well.
3. Serve immediately and refrigerate any leftovers.

Nutrition Information

- Calories: 192
- Fat: 4 g
- Saturated fat: 1 g
- Trans fat: 0 g
- Carbohydrates: 32 g
- Sugar: 6 g
- Sodium: 1297 mg
- Fiber: 8 g
- Protein: 10 g
- Cholesterol: 4 mg

Delicious Zucchini Noodles With Garlic Salmon

Serve: 4

Free Style Smart Points: 2

Ingredients

- 1.33 lbs wild salmon fillets (skinless if possible)
- 2 tsp. smoked paprika
- 1/2 tsp. salt
- 1/2 tsp. garlic powder
- 1/4 tsp. pepper
- 1/4 tsp. onion powder
- 1/4 tsp. dried oregano
- 1/8 tsp. chili powder (more to taste)
- 2 tbsp. olive oil, divided
- 2 zucchini, cut into noodles
- 1 cup cherry tomatoes
- 2 garlic cloves, minced
- 1 lemon

Instructions:

1.	Mix together the smoked paprika, salt, garlic powder, pepper, onion powder, oregano, and chili powder. Pat the salmon dry using a paper towel and press the spice mixture onto the salmon on both sides. (If you salmon has skin, just coat one side of the fish.)

2.	Prepare your zucchini noodles using a spiralizer, sharp knife, or vegetable peeler. If time permits, sprinkle the zucchini noodles with salt and place in a colander. This will remove some of the moisture and result in a firmer noodle.

3.	Heat half the olive oil over medium high heat in a heavy skillet. Cook the salmon for 3-4 minutes per side. Remove from the pan and set aside. Tent with foil to keep warm.

4.	Add the remaining olive oil to the pan along with the garlic. Cook for 1 minute. Add the zucchini noodles and tomatoes. Cook for 3-5 minutes until al dente. Season with salt and pepper.

5.	Serve salmon over the zucchini noodles with lemon.

Nutrition Information:

Calories 331

Saturated Fat 3g

Carbs 10g

Fiber 3g

Sugars 5g

Protein 36g

Paprika Egg Chicken Baked

Serve:4

Free Style Smartpoints: 2

Ingredients:

- 4 teaspoons flour
- ½ teaspoon paprika
- 1.25 lbs raw boneless skinless chicken breast tenderloins
- 2 egg whites, beaten
- ½ cup cornflake crumbs
- ½ teaspoon dried parsley flakes
- ½ teaspoon salt
- ¼ teaspoon black pepper
- ¼ teaspoon cayenne pepper
- ¼ teaspoon onion powder
- ¼ teaspoon garlic powder

Instructions:

Pre-heat the oven to 375 degrees. Line a baking sheet with parchment paper and set aside.

In a small dish, mix together the flour and paprika. Place the chicken strips into a gallon Ziploc bag and add the flour/paprika mixture. Seal the bag and shake to coat the chicken.

In a shallow dish, beat the egg whites and set aside. In a separate shallow dish, stir together the cornflake crumbs, parsley, salt, pepper, cayenne, onion powder and garlic powder.

One at a time, take the flour-coated chicken strips and coat them in the egg whites and then press them into the dish of corn flake crumbs and flip so that both sides are coated in crumbs. Transfer the crumb-coated strips to the prepared baking sheet.

When all the chicken tenders are coated and on the baking sheet, spray the tops of them with cooking spray and place in the oven to bake for 18-20 minutes until cooked through.

Nutrition Information:

229 calories,

12 g carbs,

1 g sugar,

4 g fat,

1 g saturated fat,

35 g protein,

0 g fiber

Garlic Basil Steak

Serve: 4

Free Style Smartpoints: 3

Ingredients

1-1/2 teaspoons fresh basil, chopped

1-1/2 teaspoons fresh parsley, chopped

2 teaspoons minced garlic

½ teaspoon salt

¼ teaspoon black pepper

1 pound lean steak

Instructions

Mix the first 5 ingredients together.

Coat the tops and bottoms of the steak with the garlic/seasoning mixture.

Grill 4 minutes on each side or until desired

Nutrition Information:

Calories: 183

Fat: 9 g

Saturated fat: 4 g

Sugar: 0 g

Fiber: 0 g

Protein: 24 g

Cholesterol: 75 mg

Dijon mustard Roasted Asparagus Salmon

Serve: 4
Free Style Smart Points: 4

Ingredients:
- 1.33 lbs. raw wild salmon
- 2 tbsp. lemon juice
- 2 tbsp Dijon mustard
- 1 tsp. fresh dill (or half the amount dried)
- 1/2 tsp. oregano
- 2 cloves garlic, minced
- 1 lb sweet potatoes
- 1 lb asparagus
- 1 tbsp. olive oil
- Salt and pepper

Instructions:
1. Preheat the oven to 450 degrees.
2. Mix together the lemon juice, mustard, dill, half the garlic, and oregano. Place the salmon the pan (either 4 filets or one large piece) and brush with the mustard sauce.
3. Thinly slice the potatoes into circular pieces, like chips. Toss the potatoes and asparagus with olive oil, remaining garlic, salt, and pepper.

4.   Place the veggies around the salmon, placing them in an even layer.

5.   Bake for 12-15 minutes until the salmon is cooked through and flaky and potatoes are tender.

Nutrition Information:

Calories 382

Saturated Fat 3g

Fiber 6g

Sugars 6g

Protein 37g

Butter Garlic Shrimp

Serve:4

Free Style Smart Points: 4

Ingredients:

- 1.33 lbs. raw shrimp, peeled and deveined
- 2 tbsp melted butter (or olive oil)
- 3 cloves garlic, minced
- 1 tsp. Italian seasoning
- 1/4 cup freshly grated Parmesan
- Salt and pepper
- 1 lemon, juice

Instruction:

1. Preheat the oven to 400 degrees.

2. Toss the shrimp with the melted butter, garlic, Italian seasoning, and Parmesan cheese. Place in a single layer on a baking sheet.

3. Cook for 6-8 minutes until cooked through.

4. Serve with fresh lemon juice.

Nutrition Information:

Calories 214

Saturated Fat 5g

Carbs 2g

Fiber 0g

Sugars 0g

Protein 33g

Spinach Sausage Beans Soup

Serve: 4

Free Style Smartpoint: 3

Ingredients

- 10 oz. sweet turkey Italian sausage
- Cooking spray
- 1 onion
- 4 garlic garlic cloves
- 1 (15 oz.) can cannellini beans
- 1 (14.5 oz) can stewed tomatoes
- 1 (14 oz.) can fat-free less sodium chicken broth
- 2 c. baby spinach
- 1 T.chopped fresh basil
- 2 t. chopped fresh oregano
- 2 T. grated Parmesan cheese

Instructions

Remove casings from sausage. Cook sausage in a large saucepan coated with cooking spray over high heat until browned, stirring to crumble.

Add onion and garlic to pan; cook 2 minutes. Stir in ½ cup water, beans, tomatoes, and broth. Cover and bring to a boil. Uncover and cook 3 minutes or until slightly thick. Remove from heat, and stir in spinach, basil, and oregano. Spinach will begin to shrink in the soup. Ladle

1-1/2 cups soup in each of 4 bowls, and sprinkle each serving with 1-1/2 tsp. Parmesan cheese.

Nutrition Information:

Calories: 272

Fat: 9 g

Saturated fat: 2 g

Sugar: 8 g

Sodium: 1268 mg

Fiber: 9 g

Protein: 21 g

Cholesterol: 60 mg

Spicy Ginger Turkey Stir-fry

Serve: 4

Free Style Smart Points: 3

Ingredients:

- 1 lb. green beans
- 4 tsp. coconut oil (or vegetable oil)
- 1 tbsp. sesame oil
- 2 garlic cloves, minced
- 2 tbsp. ginger, minced
- 1.33 lbs. 99% lean ground turkey
- 4 tbsp. low sodium soy sauce
- 2 tbsp. rice vinegar
- 2 tsp. Asian chili garlic paste

Instructions:

1.   Preheat the oven to broil. Toss the green beans with half of the coconut oil. Lay flat on a baking sheet covered in foil. Broil for 6-8 minutes until tender and beginning to char. Shake the pan once during cooking.

2.   Meanwhile, heat the remaining coconut and sesame oil over medium high heat. Add the ground turkey, garlic, and ginger. Brown until turkey is fully cooked.

3.   Add the green beans to the pan and stir. Then add the soy sauce, rice vinegar, and sambal olek. Cook for 1 minute. Taste and season with additional soy sauce if needed

Nutrition Information:

Calories 331

Saturated Fat 3g

Fiber 3g

Sugars 6g

Protein 36g

Garlic Chicken Marsala MeatBall

Serve: 5

Free Style Smart Points: 5

Ingredients:

- 8 ounces sliced cremini mushrooms, divided
- 1 pound 93% lean ground chicken
- 1/3 cup whole wheat seasoned or gluten-free bread crumbs
- 1/4 cup grated Pecorino cheese
- 1 large egg, beaten
- 3 garlic cloves, minced
- 2 tablespoons chopped fresh parsley, plus more for garnish
- 1 teaspoon Kosher salt
- Freshly ground black pepper
- 1/2 tablespoon all-purpose flour
- 1/2 tablespoon unsalted butter
- 1/4 cup finely chopped shallots
- 3 ounces sliced shiitake mushrooms
- 1/3 cup Marsala wine
- 3/4 cup reduced sodium chicken broth

Instructions:

1. Preheat the oven to 400F.
2. Finely chop half of the Cremini mushrooms and transfer to a medium bowl with the ground

chicken, breadcrumbs, Pecorino, egg, 1 clove of the minced garlic, parsley, 1 teaspoon kosher salt and black pepper, to taste.

3. Gently shape into 25 small meatballs, bake 15 to 18 minutes, until golden.

4. In a small bowl whisk the flour with the Marsala wine and broth.

5. Heat a large skillet on medium heat.

6. Add the butter, garlic and shallots and cook until soft and golden, about 2 minutes.

7. Add the mushrooms, season with 1/8 teaspoon salt and a pinch of black pepper, and cook, stirring occasionally, until golden, about 5 minutes.

8. Return the meatballs to the pot, pour the Marsala wine mixture over the meatballs, cover and cook 10 minutes. Garnish with parsley.

Nutrition information:
- Calories: 248
- Total Fat: 4g
- Saturated Fat: 4g
- Cholesterol: 121mg
- Sodium: 580mg
- Carbohydrates: 13g
- Fiber: 1.5g
- Sugar: 4.5g
- Protein: 21g

Smoked Ham & Apricot Dijon Glaze

Yield: 16, Serving Size: 3 ounces

Free Style Smart Points: 5

Ingredients:

- 1 (6 to 7 pound) Hickory smoked fully cooked spiral cut ham
- 5 tbsp. apricot preserves
- 2 tablespoons Dijon mustard

Directions:

1. Make the glaze: Whisk 4 tablespoons of preserves and mustard together.

2. Place the ham in a 6-quart or larger slow cooker, making sure you can put the lid on. You may have to turn the ham on its side if your ham is too large. Brush the glaze over the ham. Cover and cook on the LOW setting for 4 to 5 hours. Brush the remaining tablespoon of preserves over the ham the 30 minutes.

Nutrition Information:

- Calories: 145
- Total Fat: 7g
- Saturated Fat: 1.5g
- Carbohydrates: 12g
- Fiber: 0g
- Sugar: 11g
- Protein: 15g

Delicious Turkey Kebabs

Serve: 4

Free Style Smart Points: 0

Ingredients:

- 1.33 lbs 93% lean ground turkey
- 1 egg
- 1/2 cup onion, minced
- 2 cloves garlic, minced
- 1/4 cup fresh parsley, chopped
- 1/2 tsp cumin
- 1/2 tsp garlic powder
- 1/2 tsp paprika
- 1/4 tsp coriander
- Salt and pepper

Instructions:

1. Mix together all the ingredients until just combined. Try not to over mix to prevent the turkey from becoming tough.

2. Gently press the meat around wooden skewers to create kabobs. Refrigerate for 30 minutes. Alternatively, you can shape the meat into meatballs or

logs and refrigerate for 30 minutes. Then gently thread them onto the kabobs.

3.   Grill for 4-5 minutes per side or until turkey is cooked through.

4.   To cook in the oven, broil for 4-5 minutes per side until cooked through.

Nutrition Information:

Calories 257

Saturated Fat 4g

Fiber 0g

Sugars 1g

Protein 30g

Garlic Butternut Squash Turkey Skillet

Serve:4

Free Style Smat Point: 3

Ingredients:

- 1 tbsp. olive oil
- 1 lb 99% lean ground turkey
- 2 garlic cloves, minced
- 1/2 onion, chopped
- 1 red pepper, diced
- 2 cups butternut squash, peeled and chopped
- 1 cup diced tomatoes (not drained)
- Salt and pepper
- 1 tsp. Italian seasoning
- 1/4 tsp. red pepper flakes
- 1 cup reduced fat feta cheese (or mozzarella)

Instructions:

1. Heat the olive oil in a skillet over medium high heat. Add the turkey and cook, breaking up the meat, for 6-8 minutes. Add the garlic, onion, and red pepper. Cook for 4-5 minutes until onion begin to brown.

2.   Add the butternut squash, tomatoes, salt, pepper, Italian seasoning, and red pepper flakes. Cover the skillet and cook until the butternut squash is tender, about 6-8 minutes. Add a touch of water or brown if anything begins to burn.

3.   Add the cheese and cover for 1-2 minutes until it melts.

Nutrition Information:

Calories 280

Saturated Fat 4g

Fiber 3g

Sugars 5g

Protein 35g

Scramble Eggs Veggie Avocado

Serve: 4

Free Style Smart Points: 4

Ingredients:

- 2 tsp. olive oil
- 2 cups broccoli, chopped
- 1 red pepper, chopped
- 1/2 cup onion, diced
- 8 eggs, whisked
- Salt and pepper
- 1 tomato, diced
- 1 avocado

Instructions:

1. Heat the olive oil over medium high heat.

2. Add the veggies and cook for 3-4 minutes until tender crisp.

3. Add the eggs and stir frequently to scramble to desired doneness.

4. Top with salt, pepper, diced tomato, and avocado.

Nutrition Information:

Calories 279

Saturated Fat 4g

Fiber 6g

Sugars 4g

Protein 16g

Delicious Ginger Kung Pao Chicken

Serve: 4

Free Style Smart Points:3

Ingredients:

- 1.33 lbs boneless skinless chicken breast, chopped
- 4 tsp sesame oil, divided
- 2 garlic cloves, minced
- 1 tsp. ginger, minced
- 2 celery ribs, chopped
- 1 red pepper, chopped
- 2 tbsp low sodium soy sauce (or coconut aminos)
- 1.5 tbsp sriracha (adjust to taste)
- 1 tbsp honey (adjust to taste)
- 1/2 tsp pepper
- 1/4 cup peanuts, chopped (use cashews for Paleo)
- 2 green onions, chopped

Instructions:

1.   Add half of the sesame oil to the pan. Add the chicken, garlic, and ginger. Cook for 5-7 minutes until just cooked through. Remove and set aside.

2.   Add the remaining sesame oil to the pan. Add the celery and red pepper. Cook for 5-7 minutes until tender crisp.

3.   Meanwhile stir together the soy sauce, Sriracha, honey, and pepper.

4.   Add the chicken back to the pan and add the stir fry sauce and peanuts. Cook for 1-2 minutes so the sauce thickens. Remove from heat and let rest for 2-3 minutes so sauce can further thicken. Top with green onions.

Nutrition Information:

Calories 303

Saturated Fat 1g

Fiber 2g

Sugars 7g

Protein 36g

Conclusion

Thank you again for purchasing my book!

I hope you've enjoyed this book, and if you don't mind, would you please leave an honest review for this book on Amazon? It'd be greatly appreciated!

Thank you and good luck!

22573539R00057

Made in the USA
Columbia, SC
29 July 2018